CREATING
KNITWEAR
DESIGNS

CREATING KNITWEAR DESIGNS

Pat Ashforth
&
Steve Plummer

GUILD OF MASTER CRAFTSMAN PUBLICATIONS

First published in this form in 1996 by
Guild of Master Craftsman Publications Ltd,
166 High Street, Lewes,
East Sussex BN7 1XU

ISBN 1 86108 021 2

Diagrams by Pat Ashforth
Sketches by Steve Plummer

Designed by Fineline Studios

Typeface: Minion

Printed and bound by Redwood Books Ltd, Trowbridge, Wiltshire

Contents

Introduction

There are many books around which aim to teach you how to design and make your own knitwear. Most of them tell you far more than you want (or need) to know when you are just starting out. This little book and its companion volume, *Making Knitwear Fit*, set out to show you the absolute basics, in simple language and gentle stages.

Both books will help you to work logically towards creating the garments you can see in your imagination. *Making Knitwear Fit* concentrates on explaining how, when and why to make calculations for the garments. This book, *Creating Knitwear Designs*, is concerned with the overall design and how to achieve it. The emphasis of the books is therefore quite different, although there is some necessary overlap between them.

They are not books to teach you how to knit. We have assumed that you already have a basic knowledge of the techniques of knitting and making up, and that you are now keen to make something of your own design.

To design your own knitwear you need to:

1 Get the shapes right
2 Get the size right
3 Be able to add your own decoration

The sections which follow will show you how to achieve these three things. It is not difficult, but to make the process even easier to understand, each section begins with advice on designing for

CREATING KNITWEAR DESIGNS

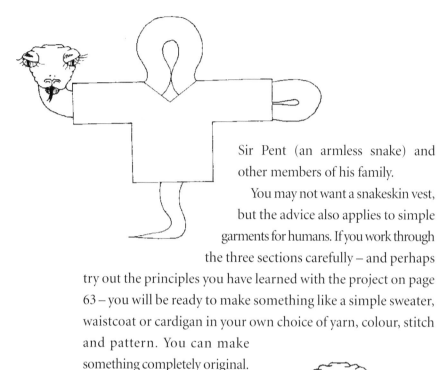

Sir Pent (an armless snake) and other members of his family.

You may not want a snakeskin vest, but the advice also applies to simple garments for humans. If you work through the three sections carefully – and perhaps try out the principles you have learned with the project on page 63 – you will be ready to make something like a simple sweater, waistcoat or cardigan in your own choice of yarn, colour, stitch and pattern. You can make something completely original.

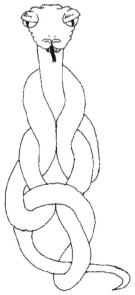

Note

The examples in this book give metric measurements only, in the interests of clarity (except for the instructions for tension squares on pages 22–3). They are there simply to demonstrate principles and the rules are the same whether you work in imperial or metric.

For your own calculations, you can use whichever units you prefer. For a table showing approximate conversions between metric and imperial measurements, *see* page 71.

Part One
Shapes

Sir Pent's vest could be made in at least three different ways, using only one piece each time.

It could be a short, wide rectangle, joined to make a tube . . .

. . . or a tall, thin rectangle, joined into a tube . . .

. . . or a cylinder on circular needles, with no join.

It is very easy to make a shape to fit Sir Pent because he has no arms or legs to get in the way.

The vest could be made more interesting by using several different colours, adding a pattern or picture, or using a textured stitch. It is important, however, to master the shapes and sizes first.

Not many people want to knit vests for snakes, but you may want to design your own knitwear. Being able to identify the basic shapes needed is the first rung on the ladder towards successfully creating your own designs.

1
Sleeveless top

This is the front view of the simplest garment to knit for any person. It has a hole for the head and holes at the sides for the arms.

Here it is opened up with a line showing the hole for your head.

It can be made in many ways. It could be a short, wide rectangle, or a long, thin one just like Sir Pent's vest – except that you would have to remember to make the hole for your head.

It could be started on a circular needle, like the vest, but you would have to split it into two before you reach the start of the armholes.

It could be made from two separate rectangles which could be two short, wide ones, two long, thin ones, or one of each. They would then be stitched together to make the right shape. There are endless possibilities for even the simplest garments.

It is not difficult to design your own knitwear from very basic shapes, but you must take time to work out how the bits go together before you can decide what size they need to be and what colours and stitches you are going to use.

The next few pages will show you the parts of basic tops, waistcoats, jumpers and jackets.

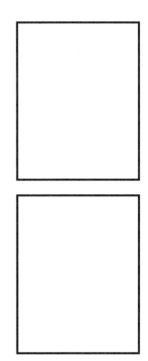

2
V-neck top

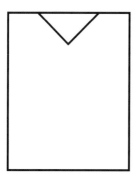

Imagine a finished sleeveless V-neck top lying on the table, with its sides not yet joined. Open it up and this is what you can see. You are looking at the inside of it.

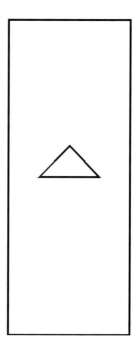

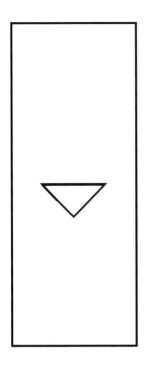

If you want to see the outside, you will need to turn it over.

From now on, when I talk about opening up a garment, I am opening it so that you can look at the outside. Whenever possible, the front will be the right way up as you look at it.

Here is the top in two separate pieces.

If you find it difficult to visualize how pieces go together, cut small versions from paper and turn and fold them until you can see which piece is which.

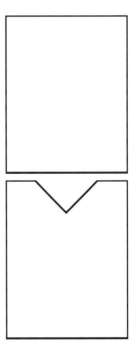

3
Waistcoat

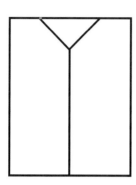

When the front of a basic sleeveless top is split into two halves, it becomes a waistcoat. It can be opened in two different ways.

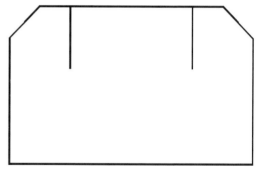

1 This way gives the pieces shown below when it is taken apart.

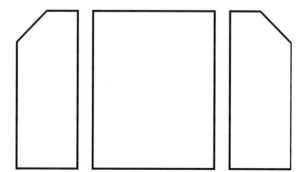

2 The pieces are exactly the same, only their position has changed. That might not be important if you are making a plain waistcoat, but it will matter when you start putting patterns onto your garments.

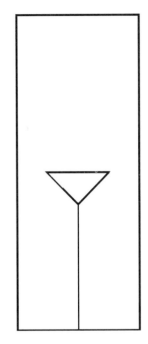

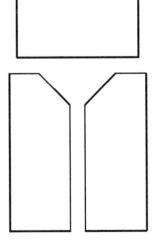

Note

These drawings do not show any bands, collars, cuffs, etc. They can be added later when you have sorted out the basic shapes (*see* page 35).

4
Jumper

Add sleeves to your V-neck top and it becomes a jumper.

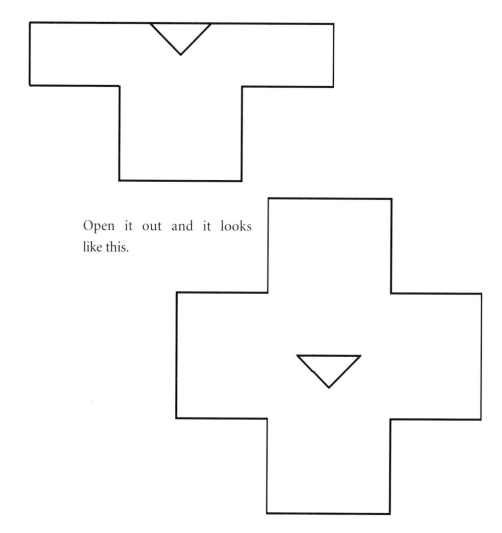

Open it out and it looks like this.

This exploded view of the jumper, shown below, consists of four rectangles, with a little shaping for the neck. You need not use rectangles and you need not split the big shape this way. This is probably the easiest way, however, and once you feel confident with it you can start to explore other ideas.

As before, you could start the body and/or the sleeves on circular needles for the tubular parts.

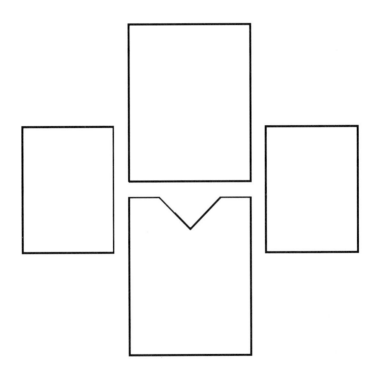

5
Jumper with tapered sleeves

There are many alterations which could be made to the basic shapes. Your waistcoat, for example, could be short and tight, or long and loose with baggy armholes. The choice is entirely yours.

One of the easiest alterations to make to the basic shape is to change the shape of the sleeves.

The sleeves shown here are the same width as the previous ones, where they join the jumper, but they get narrower towards the cuffs.

Note

All necklines are shown as V-necks in the diagrams, but that is only so that you can tell the difference between back and front. You choose your own shape. These suggestions are only to demonstrate the basic principles and start you on your way.

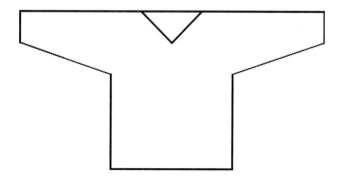

This jumper splits into the following parts.

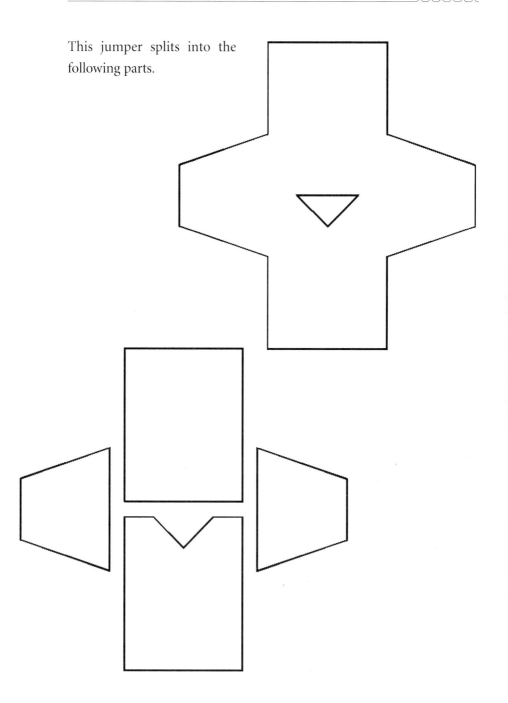

6
Jacket

Add sleeves to your waistcoat and it becomes a jacket or cardigan.

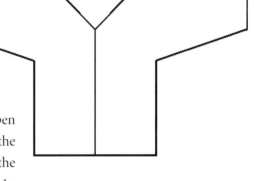

Detatch the sleeves and open it up. You can split up the pieces in the same way as the waistcoat on pages 10 and 11:

1

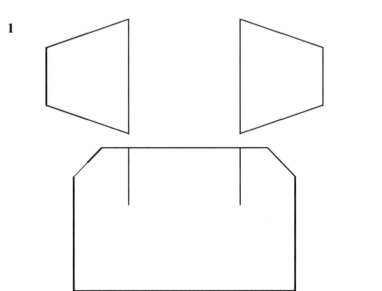

2

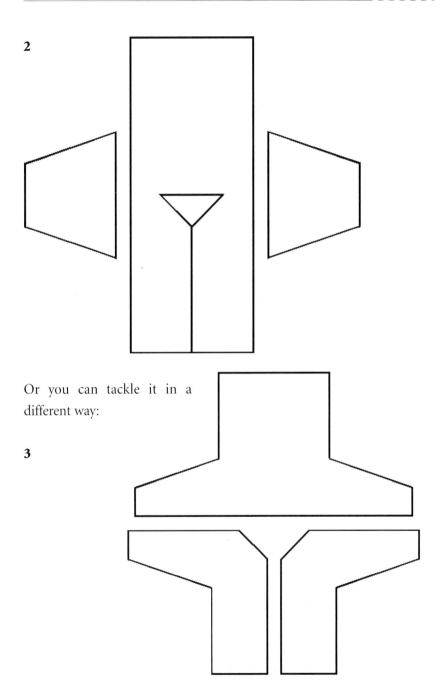

Or you can tackle it in a
different way:

3

7
Other shapes

Rectangles make your calculations easy, but you can use other shapes as well, as in the following example:

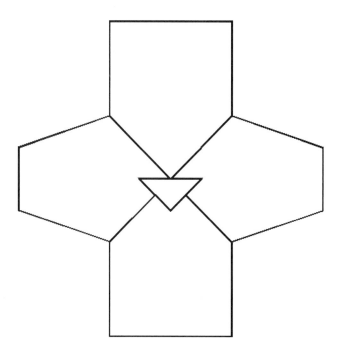

By making the sleeves narrower, the jumper starts to take on the traditional raglan appearance shown on page 19.

Knitting is very flexible. It does not need lots of shaping to make it fit. When you are more experienced, you can try making garments with complicated shaping. Until then, concentrate on making simple pieces accurately.

You would not be reading this book if you did not already have ideas of your own that you would like to use. Try out those ideas on pieces that can be made to fit together in a flat shape, which can then be folded and stitched to make the garment you want.

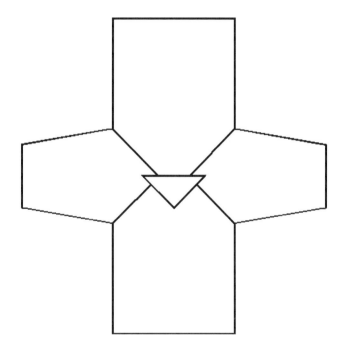

When you know which edges have to fit together, it is easy to work out the size they have to be. The next section will tell you how to achieve the correct sizes for some very simple shapes.

Part Two
Sizes

Imagine you are going to make a closely-fitting vest for Sir Pent. There are only two measurements you need to know: the distance around his body and the length he would like the vest to be.

I usually work in centimetres, and the sample measurements shown below are in centimetres. You could work in inches if you prefer. The rules are exactly the same, but do not change part way through a garment, or the pieces might not fit together.

Sir Pent's vital statistics are as follows:

Distance around his body = 42cm
Length of vest = 65cm

If the vest is to be made in one piece, you have three main choices:

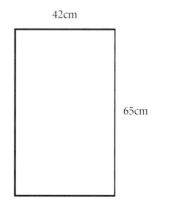

1 A tube (right)
2 A short, wide rectangle (below left)
3 A tall, thin rectangle (below right)

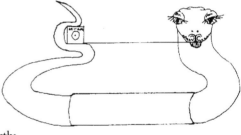

The tube will fit if it is made exactly to Sir Pent's measurements. Both rectangles will need to be a tiny bit bigger on the (long) edges that join together, to allow for the stitching up.

42cm

65cm

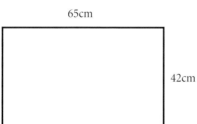

42cm

65cm

8
Calculating tension

Choose your yarn
Use any yarn for any garment, if you think it is suitable.

Choose your needles
Try knitting the yarn with various needle sizes until your work has the feel you like.

Working in inches?
Following the same method as for centimetres: knit an 8in square; cut a 4in hole; divide by 4.

Count the rows and stitches
How many rows can you see? How many stitches in the rows? Include part rows and stitches.

Find how many rows and stitches make 1cm
Divide the number of rows by 10. (This is how many rows you need for each centimetre.)
Divide the number of stitches by 10. (This is how many stitches you need for each centimetre.)
Be accurate: do not ignore the decimal part of the number.

Before you can go any further, you must make some decisions about the yarn, needles and stitch you are going to use. Starting at the snake's head, follow the instructions along his body. These will tell you exactly what to do to calculate tension accurately.

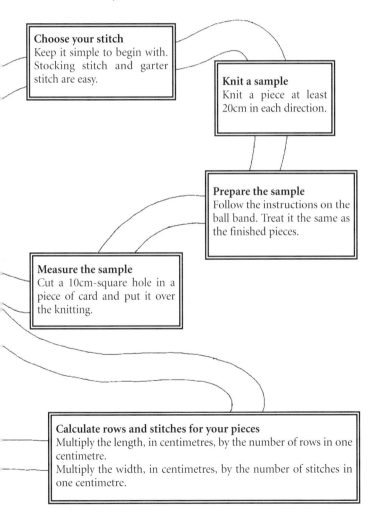

Choose your stitch
Keep it simple to begin with. Stocking stitch and garter stitch are easy.

Knit a sample
Knit a piece at least 20cm in each direction.

Prepare the sample
Follow the instructions on the ball band. Treat it the same as the finished pieces.

Measure the sample
Cut a 10cm-square hole in a piece of card and put it over the knitting.

Calculate rows and stitches for your pieces
Multiply the length, in centimetres, by the number of rows in one centimetre.
Multiply the width, in centimetres, by the number of stitches in one centimetre.

Now to continue with Sir Pent's vest.

Example 1

If a 10cm sample has 21 stitches and 27 rows, that means each centimetre has 2.1 stitches and 2.7 rows.

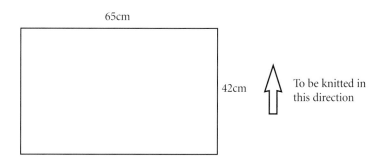

65cm

42cm

To be knitted in this direction

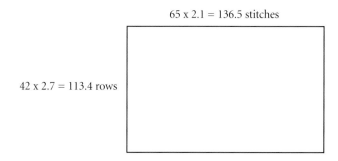

65 x 2.1 = 136.5 stitches

42 x 2.7 = 113.4 rows

You cannot knit part stitches, so make 136 or 137.

One row will disappear inside the seam when you join the rectangle and you must have a whole number of rows, so knit 114 or 115 rows.

Example 2

If a 10cm sample has 13 stitches and 19 rows, that means each centimetre has 1.3 stitches and 1.9 rows.

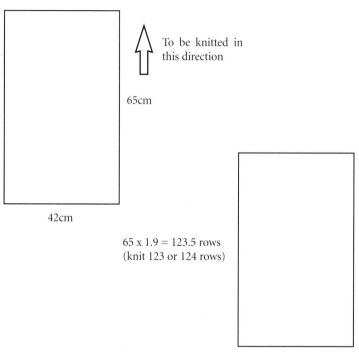

To be knitted in this direction

65cm

42cm

65 x 1.9 = 123.5 rows
(knit 123 or 124 rows)

42 x 1.3 = 54.6 stitches
(the piece will join along the long edge, and some stitches will go into the seam, so cast on 56 or 57)

Tubular vest

If you prefer to knit a tube, work out the number of stitches needed for the narrow edge and knit them on a circular needle. Do not add any extra stitches because there are no joins to be made.

9
Measurements

Humans' clothes are more complicated than Sir Pent's vest and need other measurements. Take the measurements from existing garments, which might be quite different from the size of the body.

You could use the width of one jumper, the length of another, the sleeve size from a third, or any other combination you want.

When you have decided which measurements to take from a particular garment, fasten any buttons and spread it flat on the table or floor. If it is being pulled in by tight bands, you may need to stretch it out as you measure.

Wherever there are bands and edgings of any sort, you will have to decide whether to incorporate them into the main pieces, in which case you should include them in the main measurements. The alternative is to measure only the main pieces and add the bands afterwards. They can then be used to make any final adjustments to the overall size (*see* page 35).

You need the measurements:

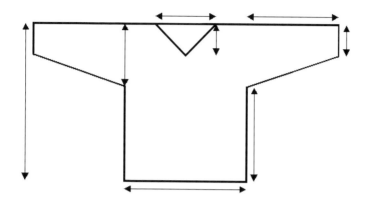

Transfer them to an exploded diagram like this:

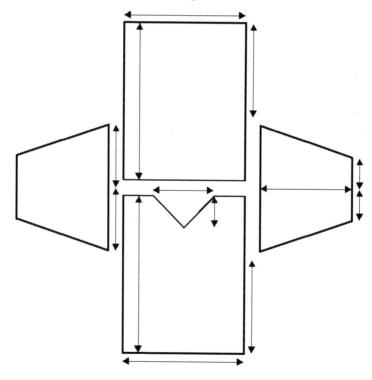

10
Calculations

Now you need to calculate the stitches and rows needed for each piece.

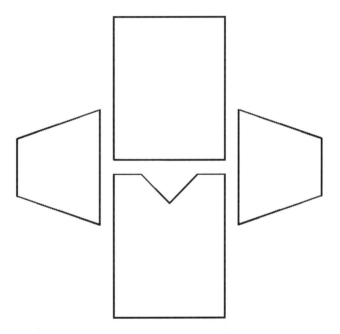

Necks

The back is a rectangle, very like Sir Pent's vest, and easy to work out. The front is the same size but with a V-neck in it.

Work out how many rows and stitches you need to reach the

bottom of the neck shaping. You know how wide the neck has to be at the widest part, so work out how many stitches that is. Work out how many rows are needed for the neck shaping.

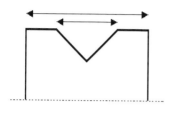

From the number of stitches right across the front, take away the number you have calculated for the neck width and you will have the total left for both shoulders. Divide this by two to find how many stitches there will be on each shoulder.

From the bottom of the neck shaping, the front has to be treated like two matching pieces which have to be knitted separately. (I am assuming that you start knitting this piece at the bottom edge.)

You know how many stitches you need to have left by the time you reach the shoulder and you know how many rows into which you have to work that shaping. What you do next depends on the shape you want to achieve.

If you want a V shape, you must decrease evenly at the neck edge, up to the shoulder. The decreases must be as evenly spaced as possible. They might be every second or third row or, if that will not fit, they could go second, third, second, third, and so on. You will have to count very carefully to decide what gives the right number.

Example

This example is for a stitch tension of 1.3 stitches per centimetre and 1.9 rows per centimetre.

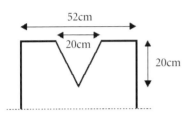

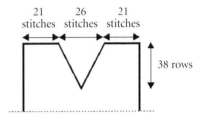

The full width of the front has 68 stitches (52 x 1.3).

The widest part of the neck opening is 26 stitches (20 x 1.3).

There are 42 stitches left for the shoulders (68 – 26). Divide this in half and there should be 21 stitches left on each shoulder.

The depth of the neck is 38 rows (20 x 1.9).

The decreases have to be worked in pairs to keep the two sides of the neck matching. 13 pairs of stitches have to disappear in the space of 38 rows. This is almost one in every three rows.

The first row will be the dividing row so should not have a decrease. To do them on rows 2, 5, 8, 11, 14, 17, 20, 23, 26, 29, 32, 35 and 38 would give 13 decreases and would fit exactly.

Another way to work out the shaping is to draw the neckline on squared paper with one square representing each stitch. This will help you to space the decreases evenly. The drawing will not look the same shape as the real neck, because stitches are not square. You would need properly proportioned graph paper to get the right effect.

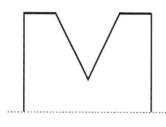

If you want a different neck shape, you could draw it full size on paper and then knit to fit the shape, or you could calculate the shape instead.

The more often you decrease, the more quickly your stitches will disappear. If you want a steep V, take the stitches off very gradually. If you want a wide neckline, decrease more often. If part of it needs to be completely flat, cast off some stitches in the appropriate place.

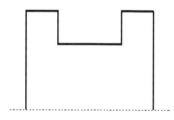

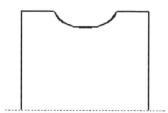

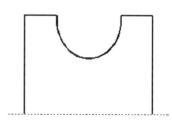

The same general rules can be used for any shaping anywhere.

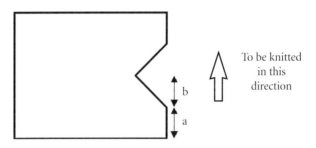

As with Sir Pent's vest, the rectangle with the neck shaping could be knitted the other way.

Now the shaping is all at one end of the piece and you will need to know how many rows to knit before the neck shaping begins, and how many rows are available to use for the shaping.

Use row tension to work out how many rows to knit before you begin the shaping (a) and how many more rows would take you to the middle of the sweater (b). Use stitch tension to find out how deep the neck has to be. Work the decreases evenly, as described on pages 29 and 30. When you reach the centre of the neck (and sweater), start to increase for the outwards part of the slope in exactly the opposite positions to the decreases.

The neck can be any shape you choose. The same rules will apply whatever garment you are making. Study the overall shapes of the pieces to see where shaping is needed.

Sleeves

If you are very familiar with commercial patterns, you are probably used to knitting the sleeves from the cuff to the shoulder.

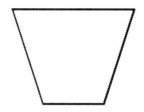

I prefer to work the other way. The measurement at the shoulder is more important than the one at the cuff, because the cuff can always be pulled in with a band later.

Work out the number of stitches needed for the widest and narrowest parts of the sleeve, and the number of rows needed to make the length. Remember to add on one everywhere there is to be a seam.

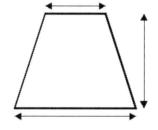

Subtract the narrowest from the widest part to find out how many stitches need to go. They should disappear in pairs at opposite ends of the row to keep the shaping equal, so divide by two to find out how many stitches you should decrease at either end. Divide the number of rows by the number of decreases and that tells you how often you should decrease.

Example

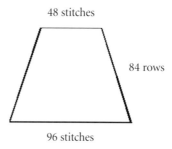

48 stitches

84 rows

96 stitches

96 – 48 = 48 (stitches to go)
48 ÷ 2 = 24 (pairs of stitches)
84 ÷ 24 = 3.5 (frequency of decrease)

You cannot decrease every three and a half rows, so you could decrease alternately on the third then the fourth rows. Or you could knit part of the sleeve decreasing every fourth row and part every third row. That would change the slope of the sleeve. With the example above, you would need to decrease every third row 12 times and every fourth row 12 times.

It is possible to knit the sleeve the other way, starting from a point, but it is rather complicated and probably best avoided until you have more experience.

To be knitted in this direction

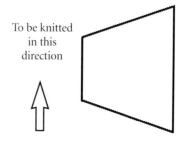

11
Finishing off

When the main pieces are assembled there may be quite a lot of finishing off still to be done. This will vary according to the style of the garment and the stitches which have been used. Some stitches – garter stitch, for example – create fabric which will remain flat and look quite complete without any additions. Others, such as stocking stitch, will curl inwards and upwards unless held flat by edgings and bands.

Experienced knitters will have a good idea of where bands are normally placed, but are probably in the habit of knitting some of them before the main sections. Most commercial patterns begin with the lower edgings and cuffs and lead straight into the main parts. The disadvantage of knitting the edgings first is that they are often tighter than the rest of the piece and so distort the shape, making it very difficult to measure. One advantage of adding the edgings last is that they can be used to adjust the width and length of the garment or the length of the sleeves.

There are many different ways of finishing edges, from binding with ribbon or adding a fringe to the more conventional 'knit one, purl one' rib. You can alter the final appearance of the garment quite considerably at this stage. Tight lower bands and cuffs and the addition of a hood and front zip, for example, can turn the basic pieces of an ordinary cardigan into a bomber jacket.

To get the precise effect you require, you may need to do

another tension square to work out the rows and stitches for your chosen edging. For the purposes of the calculations, treat the edgings as separate pieces. You can then either work them separately and stitch them on to the main pieces, or you can pick up the appropriate number of stitches from the main parts and knit on the required number of rows.

Cuffs and neck bands cause particular problems, because they must be big enough to go over the hands or head, not just big enough to go round the wrists or neck. These bands usually match the lower edging (although they do not have to), so it is a good idea to knit one of the other bands first and use it to find the size needed for the neck and wrist. Pin the band together in the smallest circle that will go over the head, then count how many stitches make up the pinned part. The neck band must contain at least this many stitches. Repeat for the wrists.

Have a go!

Now you know how to design basic garments, practise the techniques you have learned. You should have some idea by now of how the sections of a knitted garment fit together and how to make them the right size. You do not have to start with large items. Children's, babies' or dolls' clothes might be a good way to begin, and the project set out on pages 63–70 gives instructions for knitting a sweater and waistcoat for a teddy bear. If you decide to make a full-size garment, you could make one of the smaller pieces first, to check that everything is working out properly.

When the main stitches are assembled, pick up stitches where necessary to add button bands, cuffs, collars, etc.

The most important part is knowing how many rows and stitches you need for each centimetre or inch. This is your tension and it will be different for every change of yarn, needles, stitch, and so on. It also varies from person to person. You must work out the tension for every new garment to be sure of perfect results every time.

Use the basic drawings and your own tension to make whatever you want. You do not necessarily have to split any garment into all its pieces. There are many other variations that are not included here. The jacket, for example, could be made in one piece up to the armholes and then continued in sections. The jumper could be a tube up to the armholes. A jumper could also be started at one cuff and knitted in one piece to the other side. Once you know your tension and have the measurements and shape you are trying to achieve, you can do anything.

You are now well on the way to designing whatever you might want to knit. Experiment with any ideas you may have and, when you are ready, move on to finding out how to apply colours, patterns and textures to your basic designs.

Part Three
Stitches

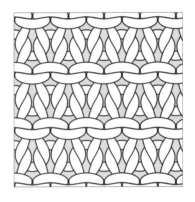

The third major element of your design is deciding what the fabric of your garment will look like. There is an unlimited choice. Even if you go for something completely plain, you will still have to choose from the vast array of yarns available. There are hundreds of shades to choose from in a variety of weights, fibres and textures. You can add interest to a plain yarn by using a decorative stitch for all or part of the garment. If you use different stitches for different parts, work out the tensions for each and adjust the stitches and rows accordingly.

Using more than one colour opens up even more possibilities. You can use as many or as few yarns as you want, but simple patterns are often the most effective. The simplest two-colour pattern consists of stripes.

12
Stripes

The easiest way to make a striped version of Sir Pent's vest is to start at the bottom edge and change colour whenever you feel like it. Because there is only one piece, it does not have to match anything else, so this random approach would be good enough.

You could decide how many rows to have in each stripe and work out how many of those stripes you will need to make the total number of rows.

The stripes do not all have to be the same width and you can use more than two colours. You can create any pattern of stripes with careful counting.

When any of the rectangles below is joined into a tube, the ends of the stripes come together and match perfectly.

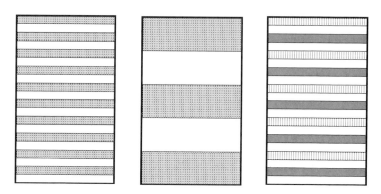

When the rectangle is knitted in the other direction, the stripes come together in a different way. This one will work. It joins into a narrow tube and the pattern of stripes continues without interruption . . .

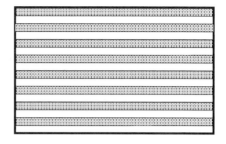

. . . but imagine what happens when this one is joined together. You would get a double-width dark stripe at the join.

There are two ways to solve this problem:

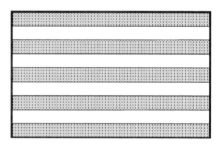

1 Change the size of the stripes to make them fit.
   This would be easy to do for Sir Pent's vest, but it might be difficult if the stripes have to match other pieces of a garment.
2 Change the size of the vest.
   Would Sir Pent really notice if his vest were a little bit bigger or a little bit smaller than the original plan? He might do, but most garments can tolerate minor alterations like this.

You could knit the stripes like this by using two colours at once, starting at the shorter edge and knitting upwards. The calculations are very similar, but the knitting is more difficult because it involves using several balls of yarn at once. If you want to knit these stripes, work out how many stitches you will need for each one, from the total number of stitches.

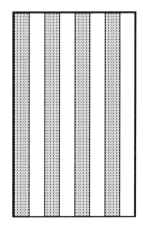

Remember that you need an extra stitch on each end, wherever there will be a join. The extra stitches should not be included in your stripe calculations, because you will not be able to see them in the finished garment. Each end stripe will be one stitch wider than the others, to look the same when they are joined.

If you do not space the stripes correctly over the stitches, you could meet the problem described on the previous page. The solutions will be the same, except that the number of stitches in each stripe will have to be adjusted, not the rows.

Making stripes fit

There are even more choices to be made with real garments. The first decision is whether the stripes will go up and down or across, and in which direction you are going to knit the pieces.

Commercial patterns often have the stripes arranged like this, but there are many other ways.

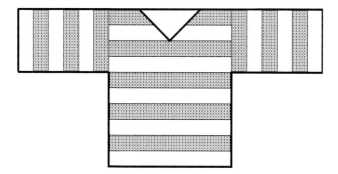

In the arrangement shown below, half a stripe from the back will join the half stripe at the front.

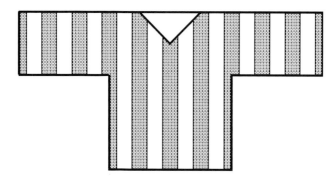

When you know where the stripes are to go, decide which of the pieces are to be knitted together, then work out where the stripes are to be placed on each piece so that they will line up when the pieces are joined.

It is not always possible to make everything match.

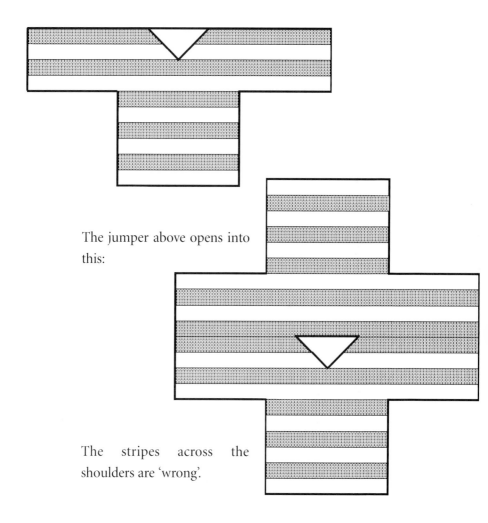

The jumper above opens into this:

The stripes across the shoulders are 'wrong'.

It might not matter if the pattern were only on the shoulders, but it extends down the sleeves and would be very noticeable. If you like it, you could have this as a feature of your design, but you should be aware that it will happen.

Moving half of the stripes solves the problem on the shoulders, but creates another.

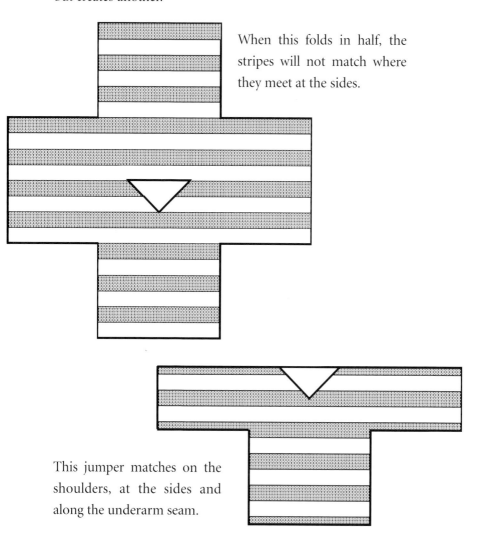

When this folds in half, the stripes will not match where they meet at the sides.

This jumper matches on the shoulders, at the sides and along the underarm seam.

If you must have one seam that does not match, make it the underarm one, as this is often hidden from view.

13
Building border patterns

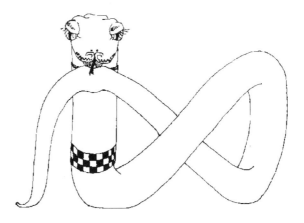

Border patterns are easier to place than stripes, because they only cover a small part of your garment and the rest will probably be fairly plain. There are still problems to be avoided.

You could be using a pattern that you have designed yourself, or one you have seen before. Whichever it is, you need to fit it into the number of stitches you will be using. If it will not fit exactly, you might be able to add or subtract a few stitches if the measurements of your garment could stand a slight alteration.

Working the main parts of the garment in one piece would give you more flexibility for where to begin and end the pattern. There would also be no more than one join in the border, so it should be much easier to work out.

This pattern has a repeat of 15 stitches. The total number of stitches would need to be a multiple of 15, plus an extra stitch at each end for the seams.

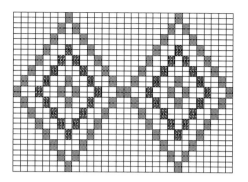

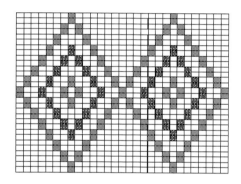

This border is similar to the one above, but now the diamonds share the centre stitch. Only 14 stitches are needed for each repeat, with an extra stitch to complete the last diamond (and two for the seams).

This time the diamonds share a 'space' between them. The repeat is 16 stitches, with an extra one to complete the pattern and one extra wherever there will be a seam.

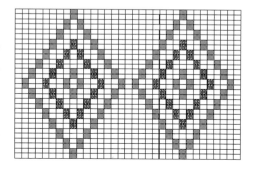

If the design is very large, or you cannot alter the measurements, you may have to join part shapes. Try to position them so that the parts match. This looks much neater and more planned.

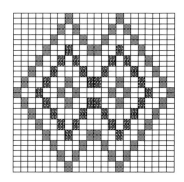

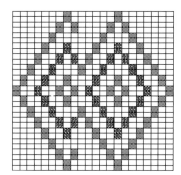

This is what can happen when two part pieces meet at a seam and there has been no thought about how they come together.

When you have to position the pattern on a shaped piece of knitting (such as round a sleeve) you will get an effect like this. It can still look neat if you think about how the shapes will meet before you decide where to place them.

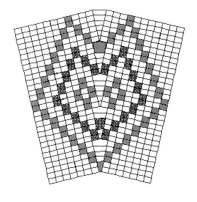

Use two or more border patterns together. You could repeat the same pattern or choose different ones. It does not matter whether the patterns have the same number of stitches as long as they all fit into the number of stitches you need. You might think they look neater when they have the same number of stitches and can line up above each other.

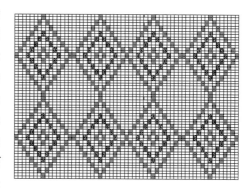

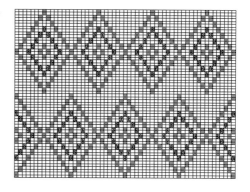

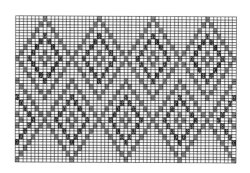

Making borders fit

It is not always possible to make a border pattern fit your sweater. For instance, if the back has 75 stitches, there are very few repeats which will fit exactly. A small pattern with a 3-stitch repeat will fit. So will a 5-stitch pattern. No other small patterns will fit because no other numbers will divide into the 75 stitches. Larger patterns of 15 or 25 stitches will fit.

> ## Note
>
> Remember that you need an extra stitch everywhere you have a seam. That stitch is not counted in these calculations.

You could make the back and front in one piece, up to the armholes, and that gives more options for unbroken patterns. The total stitches, for back and front together, would be 150. This divides by 2, 6, 10 and 30, in addition to the repeats already mentioned.

Even if your pattern does fit exactly, the precise positioning needs careful planning. Your sweater could look very odd if the design is unintentionally off-centre. Squared paper will again be useful, although you might need to use very large pieces. The squares on the paper might be bigger than the stitches in your knitting, so the drawing could turn out larger than life size. Ordinary graph paper works well for this type of planning. It will show you clearly whether the pattern will fit, although the proportions will not look right: a square on the paper will be a rectangle on the knitting.

If you really want to use a pattern which will not fit easily, think even more carefully about the positioning. For example, a 16-stitch repeat will not fit into the 75-stitch back, or into the

150-stitch total. Some other solution needs to be found. Spacing out the patterns does not seem to be an option, because the next size which would fit would be 25 stitches and this would leave large gaps between the patterns.

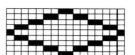

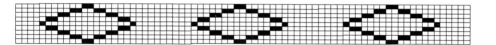

Overlapping the patterns slightly would make a 15-stitch repeat, which would fit. That does not matter on a pattern like the one illustrated, but it would matter if you were trying to overlap writing or part of a picture.

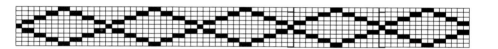

Using the 16-stitch repeat without careful positioning might result in this lop-sided effect:

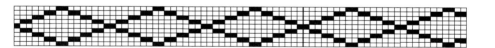

Try positioning it with the centre of a motif in the centre of the back . . .

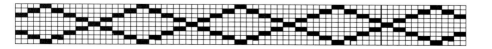

. . . or with a motif either side of the centre back.

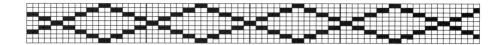

In either case, the edges will not have complete motifs, but the front will match the back where they meet. The two edges are not identical, because the row has an odd number of stitches. Adding a stitch to one end would correct this.

Once you have worked out the position across the jumper, it is easy to line up more repeats above it . . .

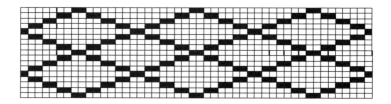

. . . or to add other rows of patterns with a different number of stitches.

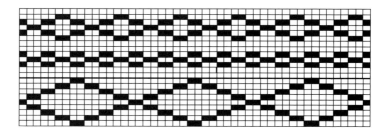

14
All·over designs

An all-over design could consist of any shapes you would like to use. I have used checks in the following examples, because they are clear to see. You might be using flowers or animals, or even a textured stitch pattern. Whatever design you are trying to place, you will need to use elements of all you have learned about stripes and borders.

Try to make the design match at every seam. This is easiest to do with a symmetrical pattern.

This one will match at the sides, shoulders and underarm seams, although the underarms would not match completely if the sleeves were shaped instead of being straight.

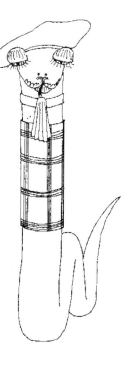

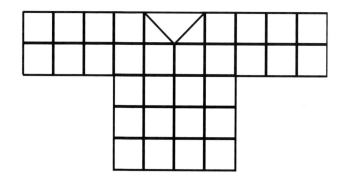

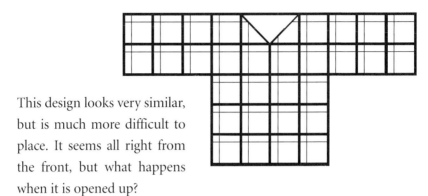

This design looks very similar, but is much more difficult to place. It seems all right from the front, but what happens when it is opened up?

If the pattern carries on over the shoulders you get this. It looks right when it is flat, but when you fold it into a jumper shape the lines will not match. At the sides it will look like this:

This way the pattern matches perfectly going round the sweater, but the lines get very confused at the shoulders.

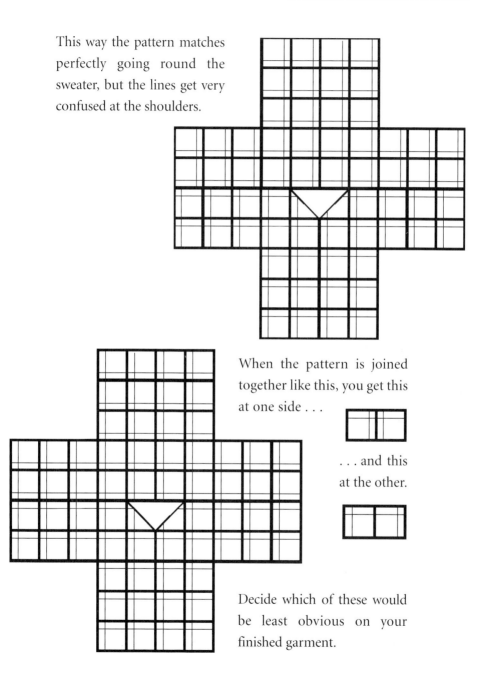

When the pattern is joined together like this, you get this at one side . . .

. . . and this at the other.

Decide which of these would be least obvious on your finished garment.

You probably noticed that the sleeves in the previous example make a continuous design with the body of the jumper. I think this looks much neater, but you may have different opinions.

Many commercial patterns tend to use the same design in the same direction for every piece. For instance, this repeated pattern might be used on the back, front and sleeves with the knitting started at the bottom each time,

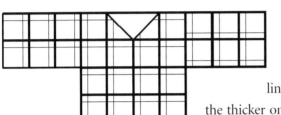

having the fine horizontal line always below the thicker one and the fine vertical line always to the right of the thicker one. The lines would not match on the finished garment.

You do not have to work in this way. Knit in any direction and position the design wherever you

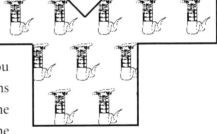

want it to be. Ignore conventions to produce original designs. Some designs cannot be reversed. The most obvious example is lettering. Similarly, some designs have a definite right way up and cannot be used upside down on any of the pieces. A check could go either way, but a snake would look silly standing on his head.

Everything about repeated designs also applies to textured stitch patterns. Patterns that do not match are not as noticeable when you are using only one colour, but you should still try to match things wherever possible.

15
Creating pictures

Instead of a repeated design you could have a picture. It could be a small motif . . .

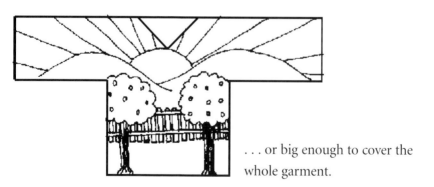

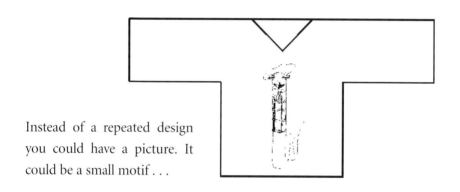

. . . or big enough to cover the whole garment.

It is easiest to use pictures and motifs from existing knitting patterns. Do not use square-based designs, such as those used for cross stitch, because your picture may end up looking distorted. The majority of knitting stitches will not produce squares. In all the grids shown earlier you will see that the stitches are wider than they are tall. This is why you get more rows than stitches to a centimetre (or inch). The width of a stitch is about one and a half times the height, and you can use this as a very rough guide for the proportions of stocking stitch.

Most motifs will fit most sweaters, although the results could vary a great deal according to the yarn being used. A thick yarn needs fewer stitches to make the garment. Each stitch is big so the motif will also be big. With a finer yarn the stitches are smaller so the motif will be smaller. If it is very small, you could consider doubling the number of stitches and rows, to make the motif twice as high and twice as wide.

To position your motif, count how many stitches and rows it has at its widest points and decide where you want to position a block of this size.

Example

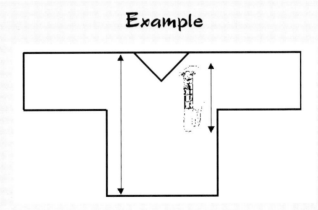

The full length of the sweater is 120 rows and the motif is 54 rows high. That leaves 66 rows plain. Some of these need to be above the snake's head so that he is not right up on the shoulder. If you have 10 plain rows at the top, 56 plain

rows need to be worked before the motif begins.

Count the number of stitches across the widest point of the motif and imagine it being enclosed in a rectangle of that size. This is the rectangle that has to be placed, although many of its stitches may be the same as the main part of the sweater. To find the correct position for it, leave the required number of stitches before you start to work the rectangle. In a case like the one shown here, you do not have to be able to fit the whole rectangle on to the garment. The snake's head follows the line of the neck and will fit onto the sweater without that corner of the rectangle having to fit.

A big picture is more awkward. It is very difficult to alter an existing picture to make it fit a completely different size of garment. If the size is nearly right but just a little bit too big, you may be able to miss off a few stitches at each side and a few rows from the top and/or bottom to make it fit. If it is slightly too small, you can probably add a few extra stitches on each side. Most pictures are set on a plainer background which could possibly be extended.

You could use some elements of a picture and miss out others. If there is no room for two trees, for example, use one of them. You could knit the back and front as one piece and let a large picture spread over both.

If you cannot find the picture you want, at the right size, the best thing is to draw your own on special knitter's graph paper. It comes in various proportions: choose the one nearest to your knitting. Use your row and stitch calculations to find out how many stitches and rows you want the picture to cover. Mark off an area of that size and draw your picture to fit in the shape. Doing this in the colours you are going to use makes it clearer to see than the symbols you often find on charts. Use your drawing like any other knitting chart. The shapes on the knitting should come out exactly like those you have drawn when you knit one stitch for each block on the paper.

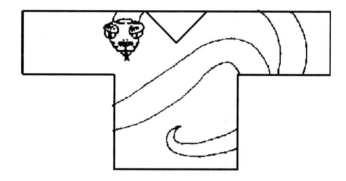

Pictures do not always have to be in the middle. They can be anywhere and can spread over several pieces of the garment. Use the garment as a canvas on which to paint anything you want.

One of the main advantages of knitting is that a simple, flat shape can so easily become a three-dimensional object. Be sure that your flat shape is right and will give you the garment you want; then you can concentrate on adding as much, or as little, surface decoration as you like. There are many more ways of changing the overall look than those mentioned here.

Now that you know the three basic elements – planning shapes, sizes and decoration – you can experiment with ideas of your own to create original knitwear. You still have many decisions to make for yourself. The choice of yarn, colours, stitches, etc. is entirely up to you.

Although there are many good books available with information about stitches and methods of construction, you should not try to do too many things at once. If you are already an experienced knitter you may feel able to tackle something with complex stitches, but most novice designers would be wise to do something simple first.

Once you start designing for yourself, you will probably never resort to a printed pattern again. You can create something totally original every time.

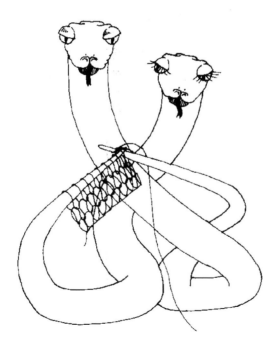

Part Four
Project

16
Teddy bear sweater

Teddy bears are much smaller than human beings, so designing and knitting for a bear will be a much quicker way to practise than knitting for yourself. Another advantage of knitting for bears is that they are not too fussy about minor mistakes or finishing details.

If you have a bear of your own, design for him, but if not, use the measurements given overleaf for my (fat) bear.

Measurements

Decide whether to work in centimetres or inches and stick to your chosen units throughout. If your bear is fortunate enough to have a sweater already, take your measurements from that. If you are measuring the bear, remember that he will not want a skin-tight sweater, so a small amount should be added on to his chest measurement to allow for 'movement'.

		Your bear cm or in	My bear	
			cm	in
Chest round widest part (including ease)		_____	54	21
Width of sweater (half chest measurement)	**a**	_____	27	10.5
Length of sweater	**b**	_____	17	7
Length of sleeve	**c**	_____	8	3
Depth of armhole		_____	11	4.5
Width of sleeve (double armhole depth)	**d**	_____	22	9

The simplest sweater for a bear consists of four rectangles. There is no shaping in any of these pieces. You can concentrate on other aspects of the design. There will be no shaping for the neck, because bears have very large heads. A hole of the right size can be left in the seam.

Note

The width of the back is the same as the width of the front. Each is half of the chest measurement. The width of the sleeve is double the depth of the armhole.

Transfer your measurements to the 'plan' of the sweater.

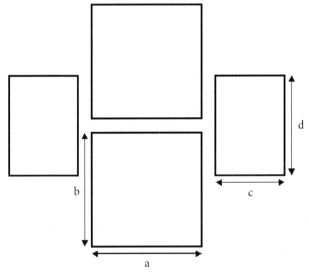

Tension

To make sure the garment is the right size, you will need to work out your tension (*see* pages 22–3). If your bear is small, the tension squares might be bigger than the pieces you finally make.

Using your chosen yarn, needles and stitch, knit a piece which is more than 10cm (4in) in both directions. The exact size does not matter. You can get a rough idea of how many stitches to use by reading the information on the ball band.

Block or press the piece, according to the instructions. Mark off a 10cm (4in) square.

Count stitches and rows

Stitches across square _____ Rows in square _____

Calculate tension

Stitch tension

Divide stitches by 10 _____ (cm)

or

Divide stitches by 4 _____ (in)

Row tension

Divide rows by 10 _____ (cm)

or

Divide rows by 4 _____ (in)

Back and front rectangles

Width = **a** x stitch tension = _____ stitches

Length = **b** x row tension   = _____ rows

Sleeve rectangles

Width = **d** x stitch tension = _____ stitches

Length = **c** x row tension   = _____ rows

Make a plain sweater

Knit the four rectangles (two of each size). Stitch the shoulders together, leaving a hole big enough for the bear's head to go through. Stitch the sleeves to the front and back, ensuring that the centre of the top of the sleeve is at the shoulder seam. Stitch the side and sleeve seams. You could add a button and loop at each side of the neck if it seems to gape once the garment is on the bear.

Add a border

If you add a border in the positions shown below, when the pieces join together there will be a continuous border near the bottom of the sweater and one round each sleeve. You can choose the exact positions for yourself.

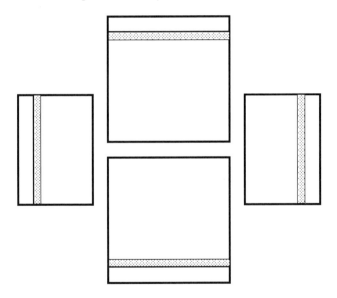

You can use your own border design if you want to, but this is an easy one to practise. It has a 4-stitch repeat (two of the first colour followed by two of the second) right across it.

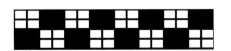

Positioning the border on the body

When you join the pieces together, a small part of the border will disappear into the seams. This may be a half stitch or whole stitch at the end of each piece. It depends how you like to join your seams. You will have to decide now, or the design will not match. I will assume that you are losing a whole stitch at each end.

The pattern will not be continuous if you stitch these together.

You need an extra stitch on each end so you need a multiple of 4 plus 2 extra stitches.

If the rectangles which make up the bear's sweater do not have the right number of stitches, you will have to add or subtract a stitch or two to make the border fit.

Positioning the border on the sleeves

One stitch will disappear into the seam at each side when the sleeve joins into a tube. Your stitches should be a multiple of 4 plus 2 extra.

A bigger border

Add a second border, with a more obvious pattern.

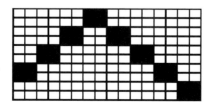

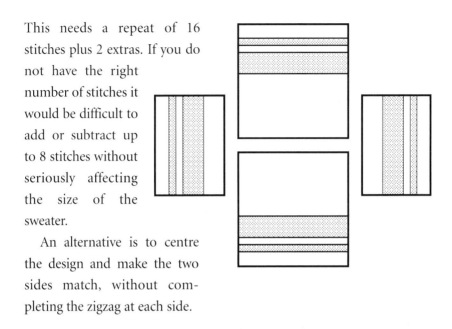

This needs a repeat of 16 stitches plus 2 extras. If you do not have the right number of stitches it would be difficult to add or subtract up to 8 stitches without seriously affecting the size of the sweater.

An alternative is to centre the design and make the two sides match, without completing the zigzag at each side.

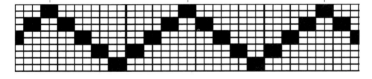

When you are ready to begin this border, mark the centre of your row and count blocks of 16 from the centre. Each block of 16 will take you to the middle of the top of a peak. Any extra stitches can be counted and matched to the grid.

Waistcoat

Now that your bear has a sweater, why not make him a waistcoat to go with it? It will need to be bigger than the sweater, as there has to be room for the sweater underneath.

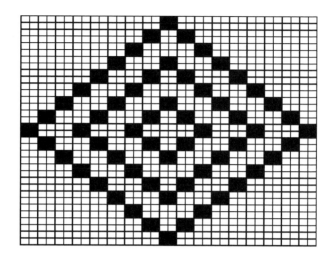

Place the design illustrated above in the centre of the back of the waistcoat. It will need 34 stitches. If you have not got that many, you could just use the centre of the design instead of the whole of it. That would only need 22 stitches.

Another alternative is to make the back and two front parts in one piece and let the design spread round to the front. You will have to make a design decision, depending on the size of the waistcoat and the effect you would like to achieve.

When you are proficient at these basic teddy bear clothes, move on to smarter, more tailored garments, or full-size versions for humans.

Metric Conversion Table

inches to millimetres and centimetres
mm = millimetres   cm = centimetres

inches	mm	cm	inches	cm	inches	cm
⅛	3	0.3	9	22.9	30	76.2
¼	6	0.6	10	25.4	31	78.7
⅜	10	1.0	11	27.9	32	81.3
½	13	1.3	12	30.5	33	83.8
⅝	16	1.6	13	33.0	34	86.4
¾	19	1.9	14	35.6	35	88.9
⅞	22	2.2	15	38.1	36	91.4
1	25	2.5	16	40.6	37	94.0
1¼	32	3.2	17	43.2	38	96.5
1½	38	3.8	18	45.7	39	99.1
1¾	44	4.4	19	48.3	40	101.6
2	51	5.1	20	50.8	41	104.1
2½	64	6.4	21	53.3	42	106.7
3	76	7.6	22	55.9	43	109.2
3½	89	8.9	23	58.4	44	111.8
4	102	10.2	24	61.0	45	114.3
4½	114	11.4	25	63.5	46	116.8
5	127	12.7	26	66.0	47	119.4
6	152	15.2	27	68.6	48	121.9
7	178	17.8	28	71.1	49	124.5
8	203	20.3	29	73.7	50	127.0

About the authors

Pat Ashforth and Steve Plummer are both mathematics teachers. Pat is Assistant Head of Maths at Denbigh High School in Luton, and Steve is Head of Maths at Walton High School, Nelson, in Lancashire. A lifelong knitter, Pat became increasingly interested in experimenting with design and in finding simple mathematical rules which anyone could follow to create original garments. She and Steve then worked together to explain and illustrate these principles in the two books *Creating Knitwear Designs* and *Making Knitwear Fit*. They have written one previous book together, called *Woolly Thoughts*.

TITLES AVAILABLE FROM

GMC PUBLICATIONS

BOOKS

WOODTURNING

ventures in Woodturning	David Springett	Pleasure & Profit from Woodturning	Reg Sherwin
rt Marsh: Woodturner	Bert Marsh	Practical Tips for Turners & Carvers	GMC Publications
Jones' Notes from the Turning Shop	Bill Jones	Practical Tips for Woodturners	GMC Publications
rving on Turning	Chris Pye	Spindle Turning	GMC Publications
louring Techniques for Woodturners	Jan Sanders	Turning Miniatures in Wood	John Sainsbury
corative Techniques for Woodturners	Hilary Bowen	Turning Wooden Toys	Terry Lawrence
teplate Turning: Features, Projects, Practice	GMC Publications	Useful Woodturning Projects	GMC Publications
een Woodwork	Mike Abbott	Woodturning: A Foundation Course	Keith Rowley
astrated Woodturning Techniques	John Hunnex	Woodturning Jewellery	Hilary Bowen
th Rowley's Woodturning Projects	Keith Rowley	Woodturning Masterclass	Tony Boase
ke Money from Woodturning	Ann & Bob Phillips	Woodturning: A Source Book of Shapes	John Hunnex
alti-Centre Woodturning	Ray Hopper	Woodturning Techniques	GMC Publications
		Woodturning Wizardry	David Springett

WOODCARVING

e Art of the Woodcarver	GMC Publications	Wildfowl Carving Volume 1	Jim Pearce
rving Birds & Beasts	GMC Publications	Wildfowl Carving Volume 2	Jim Pearce
rving Realistic Birds	David Tippey	Woodcarving: A Complete Course	Ron Butterfield
rving on Turning	Chris Pye	Woodcarving for Beginners: Projects, Techniques & Tools	
corative Woodcarving	Jeremy Williams		GMC Publications
actical Tips for Turners & Carvers	GMC Publications	Woodcarving Tools, Materials & Equipment	Chris Pye

PLANS, PROJECTS, TOOLS & THE WORKSHOP

More Woodworking Plans & Projects	GMC Publications	Sharpening: The Complete Guide	Jim Kingshott
ctric Woodwork: Power Tool Woodworking	Jeremy Broun	Sharpening Pocket Reference Book	Jim Kingshott
e Incredible Router	Jeremy Broun	Woodworking Plans & Projects	GMC Publications
king & Modifying Woodworking Tools	Jim Kingshott	The Workshop	Jim Kingshott

TOYS & MINIATURES

signing & Making Wooden Toys	Terry Kelly	Making Wooden Toys & Games	Jeff & Jennie Loader
raldic Miniature Knights	Peter Greenhill	Miniature Needlepoint Carpets	Janet Granger
king Board, Peg & Dice Games	Jeff & Jennie Loader	Restoring Rocking Horses	Clive Green & Anthony Dew
king Little Boxes from Wood	John Bennett	Turning Miniatures in Wood	John Sainsbury
king Unusual Miniatures	Graham Spalding	Turning Wooden Toys	Terry Lawrence

CREATIVE CRAFTS

e Complete Pyrography	Stephen Poole	Creating Knitwear Designs	Pat Ashforth & Steve Plummer
oss Stitch on Colour	Sheena Rogers	Making Knitwear Fit	Pat Ashforth & Steve Plummer
broidery Tips & Hints	Harold Hayes	Miniature Needlepoint Carpets	Janet Granger
		Tatting Collage	Lindsay Rogers

UPHOLSTERY AND FURNITURE

Care & Repair	*GMC Publications*	Making Fine Furniture	*Tom Darby*
Complete Woodfinishing	*Ian Hosker*	Making Shaker Furniture	*Barry Jackson*
Furniture Projects	*Rod Wales*	Seat Weaving (Practical Crafts)	*Ricky Holdstock*
Furniture Restoration (Practical Crafts)	*Kevin Jan Bonner*	Upholsterer's Pocket Reference Book	*David James*
Furniture Restoration & Repair for Beginners	*Kevin Jan Bonner*	Upholstery: A Complete Course	*David James*
Green Woodwork	*Mike Abbott*	Upholstery: Techniques & Projects	*David James*
		Woodfinishing Handbook (Practical Crafts)	*Ian Hosker*

DOLLS' HOUSES & DOLLS' HOUSE FURNITURE

Architecture for Dolls' Houses	*Joyce Percival*	Making Period Dolls' House Accessories	*Andrea Barham*
The Complete Dolls' House Book	*Jean Nisbett*	Making Period Dolls' House Furniture	*Derek & Sheila Rowbottom*
Easy-to-Make Dolls' House Accessories	*Andrea Barham*	Making Tudor Dolls' Houses	*Derek Rowbottom*
Make Your Own Dolls' House Furniture	*Maurice Harper*	Making Victorian Dolls' House Furniture	*Patricia King*
Making Dolls' House Furniture	*Patricia King*	Miniature Needlepoint Carpets	*Janet Granger*
Making Georgian Dolls' Houses	*Derek Rowbottom*	The Secrets of the Dolls' House Makers	*Jean Nisbett*

OTHER BOOKS

Guide to Marketing	*GMC Publications*	Woodworkers' Career & Educational Source Book	*GMC Publications*

VIDEOS

Carving a Figure: The Female Form	*Ray Gonzalez*	Elliptical Turning	*David Springett*
The Traditional Upholstery Workshop		Woodturning Wizardry	*David Springett*
Part 1: *Drop-in & Pinstuffed Seats*	*David James*	Turning Between Centres: The Basics	*Dennis White*
The Traditional Upholstery Workshop		Turning Bowls	*Dennis White*
Part 2: *Stuffover Upholstery*	*David James*	Boxes, Goblets & Screw Threads	*Dennis White*
Hollow Turning	*John Jordan*	Novelties & Projects	*Dennis White*
Bowl Turning	*John Jordan*	Classic Profiles	*Dennis White*
Sharpening Turning & Carving Tools	*Jim Kingshott*	Twists & Advanced Turning	*Dennis White*
Sharpening the Professional Way	*Jim Kingshott*		

MAGAZINES

WOODTURNING ● WOODCARVING ● BUSINESSMATTERS

The above represents a full list of all titles currently published or scheduled to be published. All are available direct from the
Publishers or through bookshops, newsagents and specialist retailers. To place an order, or to obtain a complete catalogue, contact

GMC Publications, 166 High Street, Lewes, East Sussex BN7 1XU United Kingdom
Tel: 01273 488005 Fax: 01273 478606

Orders by credit card are accepted